LATIN

By S.L. Hamilton

VISIT US AT
ABDOPUBLISHING.COM

Published by ABDO Publishing Company, 8000 West 78th Street, Suite 310, Edina, MN 55439. Copyright ©2011 by Abdo Consulting Group, Inc. International copyrights reserved in all countries. No part of this book may be reproduced in any form without written permission from the publisher. A&D Xtreme™ is a trademark and logo of ABDO Publishing Company.

Printed in the United States of America, North Mankato, Minnesota.
112010
012011

 PRINTED ON RECYCLED PAPER

Editor: John Hamilton
Graphic Design: Sue Hamilton
Cover Design: John Hamilton
Cover Photo: iStockphoto
Interior Photos: Alamy-pgs 13, 24 & 25; AP-pgs 11, 19, & 22; Carol Kaelson/ABC via Getty Images-pg 28; Corbis-pgs 4, 5, 8, 9, 12, 23, 24, 26, 30 & 31; Getty Images-pgs 7, 10, 14, 16, 20, 21, 23, 29, & 32; Granger Collection-pg 6; iStockphoto-pg 1; Kelsey McNeal/ABC via Getty Images-pgs 15 & 17; Thinkstock-pgs 2, 3, 26 & 27.

CONTENTS

XTREME

LATIN DANCE

Latin dances reflect the beauty and excitement of the people and music of the area surrounding the Caribbean.

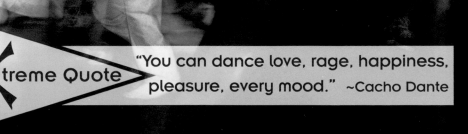

Xtreme Quote

"You can dance love, rage, happiness, pleasure, every mood." ~Cacho Dante

LATIN DANCE

Folk dances from Latin America, including Puerto Rico and Cuba, grew into today's Latin dances. In the early and mid-1900s, faster musical rhythms changed classic steps into spicy, romantic dances.

HISTORY

"The history of Latin music and dance is shaped by people; very passionate people."

DANCE

Argentine Tango

Argentine Tango was created in the South American countries of Argentina and Uruguay. Dancers move with their chests closer than their hips, often in a tight embrace. It is considered a very sultry style of dancing.

8

STYLES

"The history of love—for three minutes."
~Graciela Gonzales,
Instructor of Argentine Tango

Mambo & Cha-Cha-Cha

Cuban bandleader Perez Prado popularized Mambo music. He was known as the "King of Mambo."

The blending of jazz and Cuban music brought about the Mambo. In the late 1930s to early 1940s, dancers in Cuba, Mexico, and New York developed the Mambo's lively steps. From the Mambo came the Cha-Cha-Cha. Hip movements were added to accompany slower music. Steps were counted out as one-two-cha-cha-cha.

Merengue

The Merengue is a dance from the Dominican Republic. It is built on the steady beat of drummed music. Merengue is said to have been created by African slaves on Dominican plantations who saw ballroom dancing. The slaves then created their own fun dance steps.

Xtreme Legend

A story is told of a war hero who was shot in the leg. He danced by limping and dragging one foot. To make him feel less self-conscious, other dancers copied his style. This became the Merengue.

Paso Doble

The Paso Doble is a dance that reflects the actions of a bull and a bullfighter. The music often features fast-paced guitars and castanets. Women dancers usually wear long skirts, which represent toreadors' capes.

Xtreme Fact In Spanish, *paso* means step and *doble* means double—the two-step.

Rumba

Rumba began as a lively dance in Cuba, but changed over time into slower, teasing moves made with swaying hips. Sometimes called the "Dance of Love," the Rumba's movements mimic a woman flirting with a man. Intense eye contact is maintained between partners.

Samba

A dance from Brazil, the Samba's moves have African origins. It is a happy, suggestive dance often seen performed by street and festival dancers in Rio de Janeiro. Some credit entertainer Carmen Miranda with bringing Samba music and dance to the United States in the 1940s.

Carmen Miranda was called the "Queen of Samba."

Xtreme Fact

One of the main moves of the Samba is a combined bouncing and dropping motion. Dancers bend and then straighten their knees to the music's beat.

XTREME

Dramatic and intense, as well as high-energy fun, define Latin dance moves.

MOVES

LATIN

Latin dance fashions often feature dramatic black or white clothing. Bright, bold colors or sequined and fringed fashions are also worn.

FASHION

Hair and Shoe Styles

Latin dancers are often seen with slick, smoothed-back hair. Men wear black, lace-up, formal footwear. Women usually wear high-heeled sandals or platform shoes, which add length to their legs.

Platform Shoes

LEARN LATIN

Latin dances are very popular. The dance styles are taught in private or group lessons. They are sometimes taught in community centers and health clubs. Instructional DVDs are also available.

DANCING

DANCE

There are many Latin dance contests held throughout the world.

Apolo Ohno and Julianne Hough won the fourth season of *Dancing with the Stars.*

CONTESTS

The Colors of the Rainbow Team Match is a dance contest for young people. Latin dances are often part of ballroom contests.

THE

Ballroom Dance

Classic social dances where two partners perform a specific set of moves. Today, ballroom often includes such dances as Fox Trot, Waltz, Tango, Two-Step, and Swing.

Caribbean

An area of the western Atlantic Ocean generally southeast of the Gulf of Mexico and north of South America.

Castanets

Small, hand-held pieces of wood, ivory, or plastic that are clacked together to accompany Latin music and dance. Each castanet is made of two pieces joined by a cord at the top and are snapped together by the player's fingers.

GLOSSARY

Latin America

Countries that include parts of North America (Mexico), Central America, islands in the Caribbean, and South America, where local people speak mainly Spanish or Portuguese.

Plantation

A large farm where cash crops such as coffee, sugar, or tobacco are raised by people who live on the estate. In the Dominican Republic's early history, African slaves worked on large sugar and cotton plantations.

Sultry

Expressing excitement or strong desire. Many Latin dances and dancers are called sultry.

Toreador

A person who fights bulls.

INDEX